How to Improve Your Social Skills

Assertiveness and How to Overcome Social Anxiety (2 Manuscripts in 1 Book)

By Johnathan H. Bentley

How to Overcome Social Anxiety
Build Social Confidence and Overcome Shyness

By Johnathan H. Bentley

Disclaimer:

The views expressed within this book are those of the author alone. The information contained within this book is based on the opinions, observations, and experiences of the author and is provided "AS-IS".

No warranties of any kind are made. Neither the author nor publisher are engaged in rendering professional services of any kind. Neither the author nor publisher will assume responsibility or liability for any loss or damage related directly or indirectly to the information contained within this book.

The author has attempted to be as accurate as possible with the information contained within this book. Neither the author nor publisher will assume responsibility or liability for any errors, omissions, inconsistencies, or inaccuracies.

Table of Contents

Opening

Social anxiety is not something that we were born with and have to accept; it is something that is learned and adapted throughout the course of a person's childhood, and sometimes, adult life.

Genetics can certainly play a role, but there are environmental factors that affect our social behavior, as well. These environmental factors need to be considered and analyzed if we are serious about overcoming social anxiety.

Our life experiences shape our thinking patterns. The thoughts that arise from our past experiences begin to pave the way for our future interactions with others.

When our life experiences are negative, our thoughts can easily become negative in return. If we are not careful, we can become enveloped by negative thoughts and emotions to the point where it drastically affects our perception of the world in a damaging way. This, of course, will negatively affect our relationships with others.

Overbearing bosses, bullies, and insensitive people can set us up for disaster in the social arena. If the situations are repeated, they are obviously more likely to sink in.

When people constantly find themselves being the target of a person's bad temper, they are going to get the message that the *person* sees them as "insufficient."

If these very same people find themselves being targeted by another person's bad temper, they will see a pattern developing and get the impression that the *world* sees them as "insufficient."

One negative person is considerably easier to brush off than two of them. That's why bullies like to get a group of people to help them target an individual. They know that there is strength in numbers. Before long, those who are being targeted can start to feel as if *everyone* is out to get them in some way.

It doesn't take a very long pattern of negative situations to wear down a person's social confidence. But social anxiety sufferers usually become that way due to a *series* of traumatizing experiences, rather than just one. In other words, it usually doesn't all happen in one day.

One of the biggest mistakes people make is that they only search for one special event that created their social anxiety. But oftentimes it's a series of smaller events that lead us to our paralyzed state of anxiety.

Walking daily with a pebble in your shoe can be more irritating than a onetime kick in the teeth.

We need to examine the major events, as well as the minor ones. But it can be challenging to figure out how to do so effectively.

We eventually realize that something needs to change within ourselves, but we are unsure of where to start.

Friends with good intentions will tell us to:

- **Get over it**
- **Let it go**

- **Realize that it's all in your head**

- **Understand that the past was a long time ago**

- **Remember that most people are far from perfect**

- **Stop being so hard on yourself**

But these points are a bit vague, and if it was that easy, we would have had it all figured out immediately, anyway.

Whether you view social anxiety as a psychological disorder, a genetic predisposition, or as a shyness issue that has gone out of control, the steps to recovery remain the same.

In this book, we will search for what triggers our social anxiety, examine our self-defeating behaviors, and come up with strategies on how to solve them.

Differences Between Social Anxiety and Shyness

So how do you know that you are not just shy?

Before going any further, it will certainly help to understand the difference between social anxiety and shyness, just as it can help a person who is trying to recover from a cough to acknowledge the difference between a cold and a flu.

I've been shy, and I've had social anxiety. However, I do not believe that the shyness led to social anxiety.

They are considerably different.

Social anxiety is worse. It is an overwhelming, specific type of anxiety that involves symptoms which are usually more intense than a person who is struggling with shyness.

If you go to a doctor, and tell them your social anxiety symptoms, one of the first things they will probably ask you is if there is a history of mental illness in the family.

Shyness is usually not something that people are motivated enough to go to their doctor for. For instance, a person with any type of anxiety disorder might suffer from panic attacks. Those panic attacks might lead the person to believe that he or she is having heart problems. The alleged "heart problems" will drive the person to seek help from their healthcare provider.

Butterflies in the stomach (a much milder feeling than a full-blown panic attack) is usually the worst symptom a person can expect when it comes to shyness. For this reason, the shyness is sometimes tolerated to a greater degree than social anxiety.

If you think timidity is nowhere near a big enough word to describe what you are experiencing in social situations, there is a good chance that you may have social anxiety.

Shyness is timidity, while social anxiety is terror.

Shyness wants a friend to ask someone out for them, while social anxiety can't even realistically picture going out on a date.

Shyness wants to meet strangers; it just has trouble speaking to them. Social anxiety wants isolation and avoidance, even though the person wants to go out.

To illustrate, if you like going to the barbershop or hairdresser, and you can do so with minimal stress, you might just be shy. There might be some slight discomfort if the place is crowded, but if it doesn't stop you from going, the problem does not qualify as a disorder.

On the other hand, if you find yourself cutting your own hair at home entirely (or at least mainly) for the purpose of avoiding the general public, this could be problematic enough to qualify as an actual disorder.

This isn't to say that people with social anxiety don't want to go out. In fact, it is even possible for an extrovert to be shy.

Going out and socializing might be something that a person with social anxiety really wants to do. It's just that the symptoms are strong enough to deter a socially anxious person from achieving their goals.

How to Identify The Deeply- Ingrained Trigger Points That Ignite Social Anxiety

While finding the cause of your social anxiety will not be enough to generate a cure all on its own, it is still an important step in the process of recovery.

When I talk about identifying the points that trigger social anxiety, I am not talking about public speaking or attending social events. I understand that you already know those types of things make you anxious.

What I am referring to is the idea of going a bit further into the problem. Basically, we are trying to identify what *triggers* the trigger.

So if you feel that public speaking makes you anxious, it obviously won't be good enough to say, "Well, that's what activates those bad feelings, so I guess I better avoid public speaking," and then expect everything to work out.

We want to *overcome* social anxiety; not simply learn to live with it.

If public speaking makes you anxious, that would be a trigger on the surface.

If the reason for your fear of public speaking is because you are afraid of criticism, that would be a bit more useful to know, bit still not quite enough.

If you can find the reason for your fear of criticism, then we have found what triggers the trigger.

Instead of avoiding the things that we want to do, such as attending social events, we need to discover where these overwhelming anxious feelings are coming from.

As mentioned in the opening, there is usually a series of events that took place during childhood that caused us to withdraw socially.

It's time to think back and remember where this all started.

When did you start to socially withdraw?

Is there a time that you could think of when you got into trouble for socializing?

I know that there was very little (if any) toleration of social interaction at school, with the exception of lunch break and recess. Other than that, students could face disciplinary action when they talked to each other in class without permission.

Were you ever a target for bullying?

Bullies like to involve others in what they are doing. For instance, instead of walking up to you to say something bad, they will also go behind your back to spread rumors, as well. This can make the target feel isolated, leading them to believe that no one is interested in conversing with them.

Before long, the target starts to withdraw. Even after things improve, the target might still find it difficult to get back to a positive state of mind, especially if Post-Traumatic Stress Disorder has occurred.

First, **you need to be aware of the recurring thoughts that are on your mind.**

Our thoughts are there for a reason, and what most people dismiss as "random thoughts," can actually be used to gain a better understanding as to what the underlying problem is.

Anyone who has ever let their words accidentally slip will know that our words can inadvertently broadcast what is on our minds, even when we don't want them to.

For example, a person who is preoccupied with his or her stressful day at work might inadvertently blurt out their bosses name during a conversation, even when they weren't even talking about work.

It could also happen when a person is reading.

Take the following line for example:

"When we were young, we felt like anything was possible."

A frustrated person who has struggled with a difficult life might actually misread the line as:

"When we were young, we felt like *nothing* was possible."

This can work both ways. A positive person might misinterpret a negative comment as a positive one, and vice versa.

It's thoughts like these that particularly need to be paid attention to. **We need to ask ourselves why we are having those thoughts.**

• Are you still reliving the past?

• Are you entertaining the traumatic memories?

• Have you failed to truly forgive those who have "inspired" you to develop social anxiety?

• Are you giving away your power by letting bullies control you?

While it may be true that our feelings and behaviors are caused by our own thoughts, it is equally true that people, things, and situations can influence our thoughts, as well.

For example, consider the young boy who is brimming with confidence, eager to explore the world. Although this child might be a bit naive, he believes in himself and is optimistic about the future. When he wants to pursue a goal, there are no limitations.

He works night and day painting pictures because he wants to be an artist.

After getting rejected at art school, his thoughts begin to change. He becomes upset, but it doesn't stop him. He tells himself that it's just one bad situation.

After getting rejected again at another art school, he becomes pessimistic, believing that he is a bad artist.

He ends up quitting the art school, and ultimately, gives up on painting altogether.

In this case, the people who rejected him at the art schools have changed his thoughts. The wide-eyed optimist now becomes a close-minded pessimist. He allowed a series of external factors to change his internal belief system.

Without careful analysis of the situation, he will go through the rest of his life not fully understanding what actually happened.

If people ask him why he no longer paints, he will tell them it's because painting is not something he wants to do anymore.

The reality is that he had plenty of potential, but chose to give up as soon as he was confronted with a few obstacles.

By only looking at the surface, he neglected to see the deeper issue. Rejection from external sources was the surface. Failure to disallow the negative external factors to change what he truly wanted to pursue in life was the real problem.

In other words, we need to be in control of our thinking.

We can gain control over our thoughts by asking ourselves what really needs to be done.

Ask yourself the following questions:

• Am I doing what needs to be done? Or am I too busy catering to the opinions of others?

• Was I more at peace before or after I started deviating from my original goal?

• Am I quitting this project for the right reasons? Or am I allowing fear to take control?

• If there was no such thing as an obstacle, what would I pursue the most passionately?

The thoughts which are caused by people, things, and situations can eventually influence our behaviors, driving us to do things that we never would have imagined doing.

When you are struggling with social anxiety and want to go out to a public gathering, but are feeling like you can't, it is likely because you are only looking at the surface of the situation.

Pay particular attention to the words that make you cringe.

A person who had a bad relationship with their parents might cringe when they hear the word, "parents."

Likewise, a person with social anxiety might cringe when they hear the word, "party."

A young child will usually think birthday parties are fun. If that same child develops social anxiety later in life, parties suddenly become horrific obligations.

This is likely because the young child is not concerned with aiming to please others. If something bad happens, the young child deals with it at the time. There is no anticipation of something bad happening.

As adults, we need to get back to the state of mind we had before we got into the disaster of social anxiety.

We hear our "trigger" words throughout our day-to-day lives, and then we cringe. But how often do we really take the time to stop and dig deeper to get to the bottom of the issue?

We need to get back to that childlike happiness we had growing up. It is time to push the past aside and move toward our goals.

Social anxiety is superficial.

Before we became affected by social anxiety, our values were more important than our superficial beliefs.

These superficial beliefs can distort our vision.

By getting our priorities straight, we can begin to overcome our false beliefs.

Chapter Summary:

• **Think back and try to remember where it all started**

• **Be aware of the recurring thoughts in your mind**

• Ask yourself why you are having those thoughts

• Gain control over your thoughts by asking yourself what really needs to be done

• Overcome your false beliefs by getting your priorities straight

• Stop reliving the past negative experiences, and forgive the offenders who put you through them

How to Get Your Social Life Back Together

After you have identified the deeply-ingrained triggers of your social anxiety, you can begin to take the next step—getting your social life back together.

In the last chapter, we talked about the importance of identifying the negative thoughts from the *past* that keep coming up to bother you.

In this chapter, we will talk about the importance of dealing with the thoughts about the *present*.

When we are anxious about the present, it is because our minds are filled with negative thoughts.

The reason we suffer from anxiety is because we entertain it without realizing it. Instead of lightening up and telling ourselves, "Alright, I'll do what I can, and after that, whatever happens will happen," we end up saying something like, "No! I can't believe this is happening! It can't happen like that. It just can't."

There are certain things in life that need to be changed, but **sometimes we need to accept circumstances the way they are.**

Life circumstances don't need to be changed as often as our thinking does.

A change in perspective is usually more helpful than a change of life events.

If you spill a glass of water in public and are afraid that it will cause a scene, perhaps it would help to **see the humor in the situation** instead of scolding yourself about it so severely.

When we go out, we need to bring our sense of humor with us, regardless of how anxious we may feel.

If you laugh at your own mistakes, others usually won't. If you take your small mistakes too seriously, others will usually laugh at you.

Since our negative thoughts lead to negative emotions, our judgment becomes clouded, causing us to make poor decisions.

After the result of the poor decision causes us grief, we convince ourselves that we were correct to be anxious. We become convinced that we should have listened to our instincts and just stayed home. It does not always become immediately apparent that the worst-case-scenario is not what we had imagined.

We need to get rid of our fear of feeling bad.

Socially anxious people can say that they are ultimately afraid of a particular outcome. But that outcome is rarely accurate.

A person suffering from social anxiety might refuse to go to a shopping mall because he or she doesn't want to deal with the crowds.

When confronted about why the person doesn't want to be around others, he or she responds by saying that people are inconsiderate and mean, so it's better to not have to deal with them, especially in large quantities.

Certain people can definitely be mean and inconsiderate, but that's not really what the socially anxious person's underlying problem is.

The underlying problem is that this person is afraid to experience discomfort.

Social anxiety is discomfort, just like fulfilling an important obligation is discomfort.

Oftentimes, doing the right thing will bring along with it a certain degree of discomfort. But the benefits make it worthwhile.

We can **find motivation in the fact that the discomfort of social anxiety symptoms are fairly small in comparison to what happens to us in the long run when we allow the social anxiety to take over.**

The good thing is that once we overcome our fear of feeling bad, we usually end up not feeling anywhere near as bad as we thought we would, anyway.

Have you ever noticed that there are actually plenty of wealthy people who don't really care much for money?

Sure there are plenty of rich people who are materialistic.

But there are many others whose wealth was little more than a nice side effect. They seem to have a way of building riches.

What are we missing? What do we need to know?

They got that way because they pursued their goals with passion, regardless of the obstacles that stood in the way. They enjoyed what they were doing, and then they embraced the discomfort that came along with it.

We can apply those same principles to social anxiety.

If we do what we need to do, the rest will follow.

When you are feeling anxious in social situations, it also helps to focus on the task at hand.

If you find it less stressful to go to work than to go to a party, it is likely because work allows you to distract yourself with tasks.

We need to incorporate our own tasks into our social interactions.

For example, when going to a mall, don't make it your mission to approach strangers. Doing this only adds more pressure to an already tense situation.

Instead, make it your focus to shop. This will allow you to have a purpose for your trip, other than to simply talk to people.

When we walk around with purpose in public places, it boosts our confidence. In return, it makes it easier to interact with others. It allows us to be out with the general public, without all the added pressure to socialize.

Of course, it's not always that easy.

What if we want to attend a social gathering at someone's house?

This is where using our imagination comes in handy.

As social anxiety sufferers, we have a tendency to use our imagination the wrong way. We use it to come up with all kinds of horrific scenarios that *might* happen.

But we can turn it around and **use imagination to our advantage.**

Pretend that you are on a mission. After all, it might be true. If you end up overcoming your fears by facing them, you might be able to help others do the same. In this case, the mission would be to help others overcome their fears by freeing yourself of anxiety.

Confident people have a sense of belonging.

Wherever you happen to be, remember that you have a purpose for being there, even if nothing good seems to come out of the situation.

For example, attending a certain social gathering might have felt like a waste of time. You didn't meet anyone new, and the host didn't even give you any free food.

However, when all else fails, it can at least be used as a learning experience. Maybe we were at the wrong social gathering. Maybe we need to choose better friends. Maybe we need to make wiser decisions.

The list could go on.

With enough creativity and positive thinking, we can break through the barrier of social anxiety.

Chapter Summary:

• **Know when it's time to accept a circumstance the way it is**

• **Look for the humor in the situation**

• **Stop being afraid of bad feelings**

• **Focus on the long run by realizing that the anxiety itself is usually worse than the things that might happen when you are in public places**

• **Gain a sense of purpose for being in a public place by creating tasks to focus on**

• **Use imagination to your advantage**

How to Reduce Discomfort When Socializing

In the last chapter, we talked about the importance of embracing discomfort during our social interactions.

But that is not to say that we are not allowed to reduce our discomfort to more manageable levels. We should not have to suffer needlessly. We should try to get our discomfort levels down first, and then embrace the lingering discomfort that is left.

For instance, there is nothing wrong with waiting until rush hour is over before you decide to head to the store.

It all depends on why you are doing it.

Are you trying to evade the responsibility of facing your fear? Or are you simply trying to do what is more productive time-management wise?

It is recommended that you start off slow, then progress incrementally.

A person who hasn't left the house in weeks or months isn't usually expected to attend a large gathering all of a sudden.

The person would likely benefit more from taking a walk in a quiet neighborhood first, then move on to a store that doesn't have a large volume of people condensed into it.

If you know that you are ready to take the next step, then by all means, do something bigger. You will have to be honest with yourself.

Are you really unready? Or are you just unwilling to step out of your comfort zone?

To a person with social anxiety, going out is similar to exercising for health reasons. If you don't keep at it regularly, you'll lose it.

Personally, I had tried the "time asking" question; the one where you stop and ask strangers what time it is, just so you could get accustomed to talking them. But my progress had stopped there. All it did was make me better at asking people what time it was. It never helped me make a transition to the next step.

It might seem like the *logical* thing to do, but it also seemed far from being the *effective* thing to do. It's just practice, and practice alone will not be sufficient.

Consider the students who study hard in school. They get their Master's degrees, but later have trouble securing a good career. They might also experience relationship difficulties, and end up divorced.

While it might seem like a good indicator that good students will find success in all areas of their lives, it is not an accurate indication that they will do so.

The only guarantees for a good student are good grades. Likewise, the only thing practice makes us good at is practice.

We need to do more than just practice. We need to experience the real-life situations that we have been avoiding.

We can still do the things we need to to, but **we will have to get rid of our rigid beliefs**.

One of the reasons we avoid doing what we truly need to do is because we assume that everything has to be set in stone.

We plan things out in our minds about how we would like things to go, and when reality differs from that plan, it can induce panic.

We attend social gatherings with the following beliefs:

"I have to impress."

"I have to be as talkative as everyone else."

"They have to like me."

"I can't leave early, otherwise I'll look silly."

If you are having difficulties with social awkwardness, it is possible that you are being too demanding on yourself.

This demanding behavior can be sensed by others, one way or another. In return, the social interaction will rarely go well.

People who are unkind to others usually have a difficult time being kind to themselves, and vice versa.

Since social anxiety sufferers have a difficult time letting go of negative emotions, they are more likely to become embittered by people and life in general.

When you are visibly distressed, the person you are interacting with is quite possibly going to think that you don't like him or her.

I have experienced this personally. I would be feeling uneasy about something, and the person noticed. She literally said, "If you don't like me, just tell me, and I'll leave you alone."

So it's not just socially anxious people that feel a bit insecure. The people we are interacting with can get a bit insecure, themselves. We act uneasy, and then they assume that there must be something wrong on their own behalf.

Other people were offended when I was too quiet. They didn't care whether or not I would "say the wrong thing." They just wanted me to talk to them.

If something feels like too much for you at the time, don't be afraid to let it go.

Leave that party and go home early.

Exit that business establishment and take a walk if you feel like you need to get out of there.

Say a few things to that stranger, then exit the scene if you start blushing.

There are no commitments in these cases.

Try not to plan social outings too far in advance. Why give yourself so much extra time to be nervous?

Give yourself several days to do something that requires a good deal of social interaction. Scheduling something for 9 o' clock sharp on Wednesday will put a lot of pressure on a person with social anxiety.

However, if the scheduling is more flexible, we can bypass much of the anxiety. When Tuesday night rolls around, you can tell yourself, "No problem. I'll just go Thursday, Friday, or even next week. There is nothing to be tense about, because I don't even have anywhere to go tomorrow."

Then on Wednesday morning at 7 o' clock, you can change your mind and decide to go that day, all the while you are not making any promises or guarantees that you will actually go.

Even while you're grabbing your car keys or whatever to get ready to go, you can still tell yourself that there is no commitment. "I can toss these car keys back on the table and not go if I think tomorrow will be a better day."

Keep that same mindset on the way over there. While you're walking or driving, remember that you can turn back at any time.

Just because everyone is planning on staying at the social gathering until midnight, that doesn't mean you can't leave at a much earlier time.

Sometimes we aim too high with unrealistic expectations.

Stop following your own set of strict rules for what the social "norms" are. Successful people rarely seem to follow these so called "norms," anyway.

If you stay consistent, your perception will eventually change.

Chapter Summary:

• **Get rid of rigid beliefs and stop being so demanding**

• **Stop following your own set of strict rules for what the social "norms," are.**

• **Realize that many people are actually more upset about you not talking to them at all, rather than concerning themselves about all the little mistakes you are making when you are out in public**

• **Focus on being friendly, rather than worry about how others are judging you**

Closing

Social anxiety can be overcome, but you have to be able to enjoy life first. We can enjoy life by not putting so much pressure on ourselves.

Instead of following the man-made rules of "social norms," we need to focus on what is best for ourselves and others.

Doing what is best for others is best for ourselves, and vice versa. Remember that most people are more interested in whether or not you talk to them, rather than whether or not you do something that might embarrass yourself.

Stop reliving the past experiences where your social interactions went wrong.

Get your priorities straight and stop being afraid of feeling bad. Doing good is more important than feeling good short-term.

Emotions can be misleading, and oftentimes the powerful negative emotions are present when you are doing the right thing.

Be creative and use your imagination to create tasks for yourself to focus on when you have social obligations to fulfill.

This is a mission. Treat it like one.

Assertiveness
Build Self-Esteem and Overcome Your People-Pleasing Nature

By Johnathan H. Bentley

Disclaimer:

The views expressed within this book are those of the author alone. The information contained within this book is based on the opinions, observations, and experiences of the author and is provided "AS-IS".

No warranties of any kind are made. Neither the author nor publisher are engaged in rendering professional services of any kind. Neither the author nor publisher will assume responsibility or liability for any loss or damage related directly or indirectly to the information contained within this book.

The author has attempted to be as accurate as possible with the information contained within this book. Neither the author nor publisher will assume responsibility or liability for any errors, omissions, inconsistencies, or inaccuracies.

Table of Contents

Intro

This book will get straight to the "HOW TO" aspects of developing assertiveness by utilizing powerful techniques to help you build a solid inner foundation, build your self-esteem, and recognize your self-worth.

By now, you probably already know about the importance of setting healthy boundaries, overcoming obstacles, and so forth. But now it's time to focus on how to actually do those things.

There are certain behavior patterns and habits that help identify us. Many of these habits and behaviors can be destructive, without us even realizing it. We need to identify these habits and behaviors, and then we need to fix them.

Willpower alone will not be enough to help us. You might have been told in the past to "just tough it out," but you know it doesn't work. Using nothing but willpower will usually cause us to become excessively hard on ourselves, never leaving room to really get to the root of the problem.

Instead, we need to be kind to ourselves, and it starts by building our inner foundation.

How to Build Your Inner Foundation

Although there are differing opinion as to what an "inner foundation" really is, for the sake of this chapter, I am simply referring to the inner foundation as your mind and emotions.

Getting your mind to work for you is crucial.

There are two basic ways to build your inner foundation:

1) Building directly from the inside

2) Building from the outside

Building from the inside is generally more effective, but takes a longer time to accomplish. Building from the inside means facing all of your problems head-on, and then working out the solutions, step by step. It can be a challenging process, but it is certainly worth it.

Building from the outside involves a *fake it till you make it* approach. This is where you would start doing the things you would do as if you had already accomplished your goals. You would act as if you were already assertive, and eventually, your subconscious mind will pick up on the actions you are taking.

The building from the outside technique is proven to work because the human brain does not know the difference between fiction and nonfiction. If you have ever read a fictional thriller or watched a highly suspenseful film, you might have noticed that you actually felt a bit stressed out from all of the tension. This is because your mind is reacting to whatever you place in it, fiction or not.

To illustrate the first technique (building directly from the inside), let's say one of your problems is that you feel annoyed by people who ask for your help. You begin to feel like your good nature is being taken advantage of and you are tired of it.

In this case, you would need to:

- **Ask yourself why you feel this way** (Is it an insecurity issue? If so, what is causing the insecurity? Are you being taken advantage of? If so, what is stopping you from standing your ground? Are you compromising your principles by going the extra mile as you help these people?

  - **Take as much time as you need to really think about those questions**

  - **Come up with some honest answers**

  - **Turn those answers into steps you can take to fix the problem**

To accomplish this, you will need to have the ability to identify problems, the vision to transform them into realistic goals, and the passion to persistently do what it takes to accomplish those goals.

You already know that the problem is a lack of assertiveness. But what many people don't know is that the lack of assertiveness is oftentimes just a symptom that comes from a larger problem. Paying special attention to your thoughts, feelings, and behaviors in relation to assertiveness and the lack thereof can lead you to what the bigger problem is.

The second technique (building from the outside) would involve confidently saying, "no," for as many times as it takes to get your subconscious mind to pick up on the fact that you are now assertive.

Personally, I think of the first technique as a long-lasting solution, while I see the second technique as a fast-acting one. Since they both have their pros and cons, it makes sense to implement both of them, but I only see one of them working in the long run, and that's the one you want to focus more of your energy on.

Since there's really not a whole lot more to be said about the *building from the outside* approach, we will be focusing on the *building from the inside* approach.

It all starts with:

• **Getting your priorities straight**

• **Knowing where you stand**

• **Learning how to keep your emotions under control**

These three elements are critical if we wish to remain confident without becoming aggressive or passive.

Since they are so closely related, these three things can also be lumped together. When you work on one of them, the other two elements often follow automatically.

A common factor that coincides with a lack of assertiveness is excessive stress.

Getting our priorities straight can help reduce much of the stress we face on a daily basis.

Although very stressful times are not always avoidable, just take the time to ask yourself how much of the stress is needless.

Many of the things we worry about never even come to pass. But even when certain causes of concern are entirely legitimate, going through the trials can make a person stronger, provided that person does not give up.

Look at the trials as milestones. Even though they are brutal, it can give a person something to look back on and say, "Yeah, I made it through that, so now I'll make it through this."

I know how difficult it is, but giving in the first time will only make it easier to give in the second time.

Failing to be assertive is a habit that is formed over time to the point where it becomes ingrained in an individual's personality. The good news is that since it's a habit, it can be broken.

The human mind will send out signals to the individual, explaining what needs to be done in a given situation. Dehydration will naturally lead to thirst, just as extended isolation will typically lead to a feeling of loneliness.

When we're not getting what we need out of life, it's usually because we are not spending enough time doing the right things.

It's time to start doing the things that we were called to do.

Interestingly enough, sometimes the things we value the most are the very same things that we spend the least amount of time actually doing.

Passionate artists devote the majority of their time to working jobs that they hate, so that they are able to pay their bills at the expense of neglecting their true callings.

Athletes stop working out because they realize that they'll never make big money by exercising and being healthy.

Lack of assertiveness is rooted in fear, and this fear is able to exist because we continuously feed it by starving our true priorities.

While we shouldn't neglect our responsibilities in life, we also shouldn't neglect the things in life that we are truly passionate about.

A good balance needs to be achieved.

There is a certain confidence that comes along with staying in close touch with the things that you are passionate about. This confidence is what will allow you to become more assertive.

A pattern I have noticed with people who are struggling emotionally is that they are not spending enough time pursuing their hobbies, passions, and making the most out of life. They tend to push these things aside in order to focus on their people-pleasing nature.

Take care of your priorities, and in return, the priorities will take care of you.

Along with having your priorities in order, you will also need to keep your emotions under control.

A major component involved in keeping your emotions under control is the ability to manage your expectations.

A lack of assertiveness can lead to disappointments, and disappointments can lead to an even greater lack of assertiveness. It becomes a reinforcing cycle.

The reason we set ourselves up for disappointments is because we spend too much time thinking about what we can get in return from relationships, careers, and life in general.

Instead of focusing on *doing* good, too often, people focus on *feeling* good. But feelings can be misleading.

Feeling good will work for a person's best interests in the short term; *doing* good will serve everyone's best purpose in the long run.

To illustrate, employees might think that they are being nice to their bosses by telling them that they can work absolutely anytime they want them to work. Taking advantage of the offer, the bosses scheduling their employees to work late every other night. In reality, the productiveness of the employees drops significantly when they are forced to work so late, and therefore, the company's productivity as a whole suffers. A possible solution here would be offering to come in earlier than usual instead of staying late. This way the employees can meet their employers somewhere in the middle.

It makes no sense for an early bird to have to work late at night, just as it makes no sense for a person who is more of an evening person to work so early.

There are plenty of people that are more than willing to work early, and there are plenty of people that prefer to work late. It is the employer's responsibility to assign the right people to the right time slots.

The point is that there are plenty of individuals in the world to fill specific roles. Why force a dolphin to fly when there are plenty of birds?

But this is what we attempt to do each time we fail to assert ourselves. By failing to assert ourselves, we assign ourselves to less than what we were called for.

To be overly accommodating is not always in everyone's best interest. That's not to say you should never go the extra mile. You just need to stop and evaluate the situation to determine what is really best not just for yourself, but others.

If you decline to go the extra mile, make sure it's not for selfish reasons. If you decide to go the extra mile, make sure you can afford the time and energy to do so.

Sacrifices are always going to be necessary in order to make businesses and relationships work. But there is a difference between sacrifice and compromising your values.

But why do people compromise their values? Yet again, fear is a motivating factor.

Instead of realizing that there are many fish in the sea, we focus all of our attention on one person. Instead of remembering what is truly important, we base our actions on whether or not a particular group of people agree with us or not. Instead of of focusing on enjoying the journey, we get frustrated by obsessing over how long the process is taking.

Emotions get out of control when the person feels a deep sense of hopelessness. But we need to remember that there is hope.

A break up does not mean the person will end up alone forever. A job loss does not mean that there aren't better career options available. Going through an abusive situation does not make a person powerless, even though it makes the person on the receiving end *feel* powerless.

Joyful, peaceful people know how to look at the bigger picture, even when it's not within immediate view.

Summary:

• **Get your mind to work for you by breaking down the overwhelming problems into small, manageable tasks**

• **Find out what the root of the issue is by paying special attention to your thoughts, feelings, and behaviors in relation to assertiveness and the lack thereof**

• **Reduce stress by getting your priorities in order and letting go of the things that aren't important**

• **Manage your priorities by staying in touch with the things that you are the most passionate about**

• **Keep your emotions under control by looking at the trials as milestones**

• **Remember that being overly accommodating is not always in everyone's best interests and can actually backfire sometimes**

• **Deal with fear by recognizing your true values and focusing on the big picture**

How to Build Self-Esteem

There is no doubt that a lack of assertiveness can be attributed to low self-esteem. But it's important to recognize the very big difference between high self-esteem and arrogance.

The reason it's so important to recognize this difference is because it is like a crossroad, and many people take the wrong turn. They get pushed around and then assumes that the only way to level the playing field is to become bullies, themselves.

Many people get confused and assume that they have to become bullies in order to appear assertive. But bullying is rooted in aggression and arrogance, while assertiveness is rooted in confidence and understanding.

By having a healthy self-esteem level, you can stay on the right path, even in the midst of all the obstacles you might face.

Acceptance of who you really are is a necessity. No one is *called* to be ineffective or unassertive, but life is full of negative situations that can throw us off track.

One reason we can lack self-esteem is because we are so extremely hard on ourselves. We have difficulty moving on.

While the arrogant people refuse to acknowledge their own mistakes, the unassertive people refuse to forgive themselves for making mistakes.

Oftentimes, the unassertive people will even internalize the mistakes another person made, blaming themselves for something that was not their fault.

The overly aggressive people often externalize negativity in an outward fashion, and while others simply let it roll right off, the unassertive person is likely to absorb it.

One of the best ways to prevent absorbing negativity is by talking it over with someone. If you are apprehensive to do so, just remember that some of the most successful people out there are known for honestly talking about the things that they have struggled with.

This doesn't mean you have to spill your guts to a total stranger, though. It is possible to find just as much relief in talking about your circumstances to a friend than a stranger who might happen to have a degree in psychology, so it makes sense to just talk to the friend.

For many of us, we tend to base our self-worth on the kind of worth that is placed on us by others. Our minds begin to feel like roller coasters as our emotions bounce back and forth between the highs and lows.

If someone compliments us, we feel happy. If someone puts us down, we assume that we are hopeless.

All these feelings are based on emotions. But we shouldn't rely on emotions alone, as they can be misleading.

The more time you spend dealing with people who put you down, the more likely you are to believe the things they are saying about you. If it's not realistic to spend significantly less time around such people, it's a good idea to balance things out by listening to uplifting music, talking to positive people, etc.

Don't neglect your spiritual and mental health.

Vigilance is necessary when it comes to being aware of the negative thoughts that like to creep in. Negative thinking can become such a habit that many people don't even realize they have been telling themselves lies until a more positive person has a conversation with them and wakes them up to the fact.

The lack of assertiveness is able to survive because we continue to feed it. If we starve it for long enough, it will eventually die.

Don't feed your lack of assertiveness by dwelling on negative thoughts. Instead, gain a new perspective that allows you to think more positively.

Watch your thoughts closely and don't allow yourself to dwell on anything negative.

The trouble is that we seek compassion from a world of imperfect people who are prone to fail in giving us what we seek.

We need to have self-compassion.

As we look closer at the past events of our lives, we can begin to see that we actually did the best we could with every situation we were faced with, considering the amount of resources, time, etc that were given to us.

We should accept responsibility for our own mistakes and admit to them. But even when we did make mistakes, it was usually because we lacked something that we needed, and in the meantime, we did the best with what we did have.

As aggressors, we lacked guidance. As thieves, we did not have enough people in our lives that were willing to help us financially.

This is absolutely not to justify these wrongful acts or excuse them altogether. Wrong is still wrong, regardless of the excuses we try to make. This is just to help you forgive yourself of anything in the past that you might still be beating yourself up over. It's to help show you how to be compassionate, realizing that everyone makes mistakes, just as you have.

Everyone has missed the bar, one way or another.

Mistakes can become contagious. Wrongful acts committed against us, combined with our lack of guidance and self-control can cause us to make more mistakes, adding to the mess.

This cycle needs to be broken.

Although negative people and situations might have made it difficult for us, we need to accept responsibility for our lack of assertiveness and move on.

Summary:

- **Don't mistake high self-esteem for arrogance**

- **Accept who you really are**

- **Forgive yourself and others**

- **Express feelings by talking about them with a friend**

- **Let go of the past and move on**

- **Don't rely on emotions alone**

- **Have self-compassion**

- **Starve your lack of assertiveness by dwelling on positive thoughts and shutting down negative ones**

- **Gain a new perspective and watch your thoughts closely**

How to Reduce Stress

With excessive stress in our lives, we will rarely be able to effectively get much of *anything* done, and that includes being assertive.

Since it's less challenging, it's human nature to take the path of the least resistance. But that's not always the right path to take. It's certainly no easier to take the challenging path when we are stressed out to the point where we are not functioning at our best.

Reducing stress to manageable levels can give us the added energy and focus we need to be more assertive.

Fear of conflict, codependent behavior, and frustration with demanding people will certainly add a great deal of stress to a person's life.

Taking walks regularly, listening to music, etc definitely can help you in the long run, but how do you deal with stress right on the spot?

A person can take a walk and listen to all the music they want the night before, only to find all of their hard work thrown down the drain as soon as they walk into work the next morning.

They can practice all the things they are going to say the day before they deal with someone, only to find themselves at a loss for words when the time comes.

This is because it's easy enough to relax during practice, but how do you keep that easy-going feeling when it's time to be assertive?

When you're in the midst of a high-pressure situation, you're probably not going to have time to practice breathing techniques and so forth.

But you do have to think fast.

You need to think quick enough to realize what is happening and how to react. Since the symptoms of excessive stress are due to the mind being convinced that there is a serious threat present, you need to find out whether the perceived threat is realistic or not.

A person that is yelling and complaining might be creating a very negative situation, but unless they are threatening someone with violence or something similar, the situation is probably not a very big threat.

Identify the trigger points. Writing in a journal on a daily basis is good for tracking problematic situations. Keep track of what happened, how you felt, why you think you felt that way, and then log it all into your journal. See if you can notice any patterns.

Somewhere along the way, our minds became conditioned to react to all sorts of minor scenarios as if they were life and death situations.

We give these scenarios much more time and energy than they deserve because we feel unable to let them go.

Problems arise when we feel we will be worse off if we let go. We convince ourselves that we absolutely need all of the baggage that we supposedly desire so much.

Many of these desires are actually false beliefs that are holding us back. We cling to the wrong relationship partner because we *believe* that we can't do any better. We put our goals aside because we *believe* that there are more important things to do. We stress ourselves out because we *believe* that it's normal to feel overwhelmed all the time.

We need to separate false beliefs from actual needs.

As difficult as it might seem at first to let go of extra baggage that weighs you down, it is actually a lot more stressful to hold onto all of it.

It's a bit ironic that people can be afraid of letting go of the things that stress them out the most.

You can probably recall at least one time period in the past where you felt content. It's important to remember that if you were able to feel content back then, you are also perfectly capable of feeling content now.

There will be good days, rough days, and everything in between. By using your imagination, it is possible to experience the same level of contentment on a rough day that you would on a good day.

After all, mental stress is all in the head, anyway.

If we are capable of feeding our minds stressful thoughts, we are also capable of feeding our minds positive thoughts.

Just as children would use their imagination to pretend that they were having an adventure while they were doing their chores in order to make it fun, we can simply choose to look at our situation differently in order to get through it.

Imagination and creativity are not just for writing fictional stories; they can be used to find solutions to real problems, as well.

Another reason for our lack of assertiveness, is because we have a difficult time lightening up. We take certain things way too seriously.

Start making a habit out of searching for the humor in different situations, instead of just searching for everything that's horrible about it.

I understand that not every situation will warrant humor, particularly the abusive ones. But instead of always anticipating the worst, hope for the best. Think of the other situations you've handled successfully in the past, and realize that it is also possible to handle the present circumstances.

Summary:

• **Take walks regularly, listen to music, etc**

• **Ask yourself if the perceived threat is a realistic cause for serious concern**

• **Realize that most of the time, it's not as bad it feels**

• **Identify the trigger points**

• **Keep a journal and track the most notable events on a daily basis to see if you can notice a pattern**

• **Don't be afraid to let go of certain things that are holding you back**

• **Get creative with your solutions by using your imagination and thinking outside the box**

• **Don't always take everything so seriously**

• **Make a habit out of finding humor in the midst of problems**

• **Boost your confidence by recalling past events in which you were successful, and know that it can be repeated**

<u>Closing</u>

Assertiveness isn't just about doing what's best for you, but for everyone. It's not about being pushy, but about being encouraging to yourself and others.

Assertive people are not looked up to just because of their ability to get things done, but for their ability to get things done in a way that helps others. They are known for their passion. It is this passion that allows them to pursue the things in life that they are really looking for.

Having the wrong motivation will only attract more negative situations than necessary. It's more than just standing up to a boss or an abusive situation. It's about a lifestyle. Once you build your inner foundation, the negative situations won't even be as much of a concern anymore.

Getting your priorities straight will enable you to stand your ground because you will be in a more powerful state of mind.

Remember that emotions do not always reflect facts. Emotions are unstable, but priorities are solid.

Don't lose touch with the things that you are passionate about, and in return, they won't lose touch with you.

<u>More from Johnathan H. Bentley</u>

To view the entire portfolio of books, simply go to the *Johnathan H. Bentley* author page, available at all *Amazon* stores, including <u>U.S.</u> and <u>U.K.</u>